I'M G   A   WH   ET?

Richard Spilsbury

WAYLAND

Published in paperback in 2014 by Wayland
Copyright Wayland 2014

Wayland
Hachette Children's Books
338 Euston Road
London NW1 3BH

Wayland Australia
Level 17/207 Kent Street,
Sydney, NSW 2000

Commissioning editor: Victoria Brooker
Project editor: Kay Barnham
Designer: Tim Mayer
Picture research: Richard Spilsbury
Proofreader: Alice Harman

Produced for Wayland by
White-Thomson Publishing Ltd
www.wtpub.co.uk
+44 (0)843 2087 460

British Library Cataloguing in Publication Data

Spilsbury, Richard, 1963-
I'm good at art - what job can I get?.
1. Art–Vocational guidance–Juvenile literature.
I. Title

702.3-dc23

ISBN-13: 9780750281843

Printed in China

10 9 8 7 6 5 4 3 2 1

Wayland is a division of Hachette Children's Books,
an Hachette UK company
www.hachette.co.uk

Disclaimer
The website addresses (URLs) included in this
book were valid at the time of going to press.
However, because of the nature of the Internet,
it is possible that some addresses may have
changed, or sites may have changed or closed
down since publication. While the author and
Publisher regret any inconvenience this may
cause the readers, no responsibility for any such
changes can be accepted by either the author
or Publisher.

CONTENTS

The world of art

What have cave paintings from tens of thousands of years ago and the latest video games got in common? They are both types of art. Artists use their skill and imagination to make objects, places, sounds, sights and experiences to share with other people. They use media from pencils and ink to steel, photographs and ice to do this.

The importance of art

Have you ever seen a painting called *The Scream* by Edvard Munch? Its colours and shapes help us to imagine the pain and distress of the man in the image. Art can express a wide range of emotions, information and instructions without the need for words. This makes it universal because it can be understood by different people across the world. Art and design have a crucial influence on what we wear, read, sit on, look at, enjoy and almost everything we buy. The things artists produce can help people to enjoy, learn from or even make them feel or think about the world in a new way.

↑ Artistic designs can bring exhibition spaces alive.

Art in the workplace

Artistic talent and an ability to see and express things visually are useful in a wide range of jobs. In business, artistic flair is useful in situations where visual images are vital, such as advertising and marketing, exhibition design, publishing and illustrating. Graduates with an art degree find work in museums, advertising agencies, galleries and schools, in companies designing new consumer goods, in theatres or films designing costumes and in designing web pages. As web-based industries grow, there are more and more jobs created in arts, design and media.

→

Art is not just for art galleries. Artwork can have a huge impact when it is displayed in an unconventional setting.

Special skills

Someone who is good at art might have technical and creative skills that are transferable to many jobs. For example, they might be able to think creatively to find different ways to solve problems. The ability to communicate thoughts, moods and ideas in innovative ways is useful in many careers, while a critical awareness of their own and others' strengths and weaknesses is often invaluable. Artists are often very self-disciplined, as they are used to initiating and completing work on their own.

It's a competitive field and you need skill and determination to make a career in art and design, but it can be very satisfying. Read on to find out about some of the career paths you could follow.

Illustrator

Think of the picture book that you loved the most when you were young, and remember how the illustrations brought the words alive. Illustrators use art, design and creative skills to make images that often accompany and enhance the impact of words in publications. An illustration can also work on its own to represent a brand of product, business or organisation – for example, such as a cartoon character or bank logo.

PROFESSIONAL VIEWPOINT

'I started my blog when I was 16 ... I had always loved drawing, but for the first time outsiders could see my work and comment on it. The positive feedback encouraged me, and I continued to produce work and share it online ... It's a wonderful way to get yourself out there.'
Emma Block, illustrator

← Illustrators might draw a character for a picture book over and over again until they are happy with how it looks.

What skills do I need?

Illustrators need to develop a wide range of art techniques and study what other successful illustrators are doing and have done. Many illustrators achieve this through an HND or foundation course at art college or a degree in visual communication, illustration, fine art/visual art, printmaking or fashion. To make a living out of illustration you need to show how you work creatively to different briefs, so make a portfolio of a range of projects – anything from CD cover designs to illustrations for a book.

Different types of illustrator

Some illustrators specialise in one genre, such as children's comics, video games, cookery books, food packaging or medical journals. But others work in different genres, creating anything from greetings cards to government brochures. Most illustrators are freelance, but some have agents who show their work to different clients. Illustrators work to a client's brief, which outlines the requirements for the job. Illustrators adjust the subject, mood and style of the images they make to match the client's intended audience.

← One of the first stages of a child learning to read a story is by interpreting the illustrations in a picture book.

Art conservator

Crowds can stand and marvel at rare, old and delicate artworks such as the *Mona Lisa* because of art conservators. Their job is to help preserve precious works of art for people to enjoy by repairing past damage and preventing future damage.

↑ To be an art conservator you need to be self-motivated, as you may spend a lot of time working alone.

— Job description —

Art conservators:
- examine artworks, both visually and using scientific methods such as X-rays and microscopes, to assess damage
- keep full records about the object's condition
- work out creative solutions to clean, support and repair sensitive objects using a range of instruments and materials
- recreate historically accurate finishes, such as mixing traditional paints from scratch.

What skills do I need?

Art conservation is one of the more scientific jobs in art because you need to know about the chemicals found in different media and how these are affected by the environment in which they are kept. You need to know your art history and which techniques and media artists used in the past. You also need to have a good eye for detail and colour, and have perseverance – you could spend months retouching one painting! Art conservators usually have a degree and postgraduate qualification in conservation or a related subject such as visual art or fine art. Work experience in a museum is very important, too.

PROFESSIONAL VIEWPOINT

'I love getting so close to a painting, to be able to touch its surface and realise that, 300 years ago, someone spent hours trying to get a tiny detail around an eye or a hand exactly right. You get to feel bizarrely close to the artist.'

Louise Hackett, painting conservator at Manchester Art Gallery

Art conservators work with different media. For example, they might carve wood to repair an old, ornate ceiling.

Different types of art conservator

Some art conservators work on a whole range of artworks, but others specialise in certain types, such as paper, painting, textiles or ceramics. They might work in a museum or they may travel to accompany or collect artefacts – for example, from archaeological digs. Some conservators work on art that is undamaged, perhaps checking that it is displayed or stored in the right temperature and light conditions, or researching new preservation techniques. Others restore artworks such as old paintings by removing layers of dirt and touching up cracked paint.

Fashion designer

Everything people wear – from the catwalk to the sports ground, and the classroom to the red carpet at a movie première – has been designed by fashion designers. Fashion designers create original clothing, accessories and footwear.

What skills do I need?

Fashion designers must love drawing, designing and making clothes! It helps to have proof of this through a good portfolio of work that shows a broad range of design and drawing skills. Many designers have an HND or other diploma, a foundation degree and a degree in art or fashion. Some degree courses provide a general grounding in fashion design and textiles, while others focus on manufacturing and clothing technology.

PROFESSIONAL VIEWPOINT

'I always think a designer must be able to think fast and react to new trends so that you're delivering what your customer wants and needs – you must remember when designing not to design for yourself but design for your target audience. We often visit stores to speak to the customer directly to gain their feedback and gauge exactly what they are looking for.'

Dulcie Dryden, assistant designer at George at Asda

→

As well as skill in drawing, fashion designers need to understand which colours work well together.

Different types of fashion designer

The main areas of fashion design are high-street, designer wear and haute couture. Only a few fashion designers have their own labels or work for the big names in haute couture, designing expensive one-off pieces. Most fashion designers work in teams for mass-market design houses, producing recognisable high-street brands. They often have to work to a brief set by the head of design or head of buying in their company, and design for a chain of stores. Some designers also go into costume design for theatre and film productions.

→

Fashion designers need to stay aware of current trends and colours. Some are lucky enough to go to the New York, Milan, London and Paris fashion weeks to see new ideas on the catwalk.

Job description

Fashion designers:
- keep up to date with fashion trends
- draw sketches (by hand or on computer) for designs and help create patterns
- source, select and buy fabrics and other materials to match the brief and intended garment cost
- prepare sample garments and revise designs to meet their client's needs
- adapt one-off designs for production in large numbers in factories
- oversee the quality control of finished garments.

Art teacher

Are you interested in passing on art techniques such as drawing, painting and sculpture? Would you like to help people express themselves artistically, and show them how others have achieved this through the fascinating history of art?

Art teachers help students to develop their artistic skills through an understanding of textures, shapes and colours, and an appreciation of the work of famous artists. The majority of an art teacher's work entails guiding students through different projects in ceramics, sculpture, painting, printmaking and other media.

↑ Art teachers can show their students how to experiment with different techniques.

Different types of art teacher

As a secondary school teacher, you would teach art subjects to pupils aged 11-16, or up to 19 in schools with sixth forms. You could also lecture in art at college and university. Some art teachers teach adult and other classes in community centres, art schools and colleges. Primary school teachers don't specialise in art, but it is part of their curriculum.

Job description

Art teachers:

- plan, resource and organise art lessons
- use classroom presentations and individual instruction to teach artistic skills
- teach students about artists and art history
- observe and assess students' work – for example, by examining portfolios
- grade projects, prepare reports, and meet with parents and school staff to discuss a student's artistic progress
- supervise art clubs and other extra-curricular activities, and accompany students on field trips – for example, to galleries.

What skills do I need?

Teaching requires patience, empathy and a desire to pass on knowledge and encourage enquiring minds amongst pupils. This needs training. You need a degree to become a teacher and many art teachers take an art degree. You then need further practical teacher training such as a Postgraduate Certificate in Education (PGCE) to reach a qualified teacher status (QTS). The QTS training is included on a BEd (Bachelor of Education) degree.

Trips to art galleries can give students an appreciation of many different types of art. An art teacher's insight is invaluable.

Photographer

A photograph freezes a moment, an expression, a scene or a one-off event in time like no other type of art. Working as a photographer often involves taking pictures of people or of things that individuals or businesses want to buy, for commercial use in publications such as newspapers, websites or adverts.

Not all photography happens in a photographer's studio!

Different types of photographer

Most photographers are freelancers and many specialise in a particular area of photography. This might be photojournalism (taking pictures to accompany newspaper reports), portraits of celebrities, travel shots, weddings or photographing food for cookbooks! Different skills and knowledge are required for different specialisms. For example, family photographers need patience and an ability to make people relax in front of the camera. Wildlife photographers need some knowledge of the habits of the animals they are photographing, such as when they are most active or unsafe to be near.

Photographers:

- work with clients to discuss and meet their needs on different projects
- prepare studios or locations and visit different countries, especially for travel photography and photojournalism
- use a range of digital or standard cameras and other equipment, such as specialised lighting, to take pictures
- develop and edit pictures in preparation for publication or sale
- issue and chase invoices for commissioned work.

→

Wedding photographers have to cope with the pressure of photographing a couple's big day. They have just one chance to get it right.

What skills do I need?

Photographers need a keen visual eye to assess form, colour, lighting and perspective. They can demonstrate this by building up a portfolio of their best work to show others. They also need good people skills to get commissions and to encourage their subjects to relax. Many photographers complete degrees in photography or shorter courses at art colleges (such as City & Guilds certificates, BTECs, HNDs and foundation degrees) before starting work. Experience is important and many photographers gain this by starting out as assistants to established photographers.

Graphic designer

We may find ourselves being attracted to a film because of the poster that advertises it, or we might even select a product simply because we like the packaging. Graphic designers are responsible for the style and appearance of printed materials and pages on the Internet.

↓ Graphic designers decide exactly how fonts, photos and illustrations are arranged to maximise their effect.

PROFESSIONAL VIEWPOINT

'The role does have its challenges; you need to be organised and be able to keep calm under pressure in order to meet deadlines. Being open to feedback and willing to make changes to your designs is also important. If your art director is unhappy with your work it will not go to print, so sometimes you have to make changes to what you believe is right.'

Tim George, senior designer at Wallpaper magazine

Graphic designers:

- listen to clients to understand their needs and budgets
- develop design briefs by gathering information and data through research
- estimate time and costs required to complete the work
- work with a wide range of media, from rough sketches to computer-aided design
- present or 'pitch' designs to the agency director and/or clients
- work as part of a team with others such as printers, photographers, illustrators, other designers, account executives, web developers and marketing specialists.

Graphic designers work out all aspects of how things will look: from the type of font, images and colours used, to the layout and methods of reproduction – such as printing. They work on a huge range of products and activities, including websites, adverts, magazines, video games, product packaging, exhibitions and displays. They may also design a corporate identity, which means giving an organisation or business a distinct visual 'brand'. Graphic designers are freelancers or work in-house for businesses or organisations.

↑ Computer skills are hugely important in modern graphic design.

What skills do I need?

Graphic design demands creative flair, up-to-date knowledge of graphic software and the ability to work to deadlines. Most graphic designers have a degree or HND in an arts subject such as graphic design, illustration, visual arts or communication design. Job offers are usually based on your portfolio and work experience, so try to get an internship in a design department if you can.

Arts development officer

Some arts events such as an art exhibition or a new sculpture trail can encourage the public to enjoy and get involved in art. They also attract tourists and showcase the work of artists. Arts development officers work to help bring audiences and artists together by commissioning and organising artworks into all sorts of events, from short-term exhibitions to permanent murals.

↑ Volunteering to help at a festival or event will give you experience of the skills needed to be an arts development officer. Here, beautiful light art is projected onto a bridge arch during the Vivid Light festival in Sydney, Australia.

Job description

Arts development officers:
- build up a pool of arts professionals to hire in or work with on projects
- design programmes and workshops to engage different communities
- plan projects and events, and write bids to local authorities who might hold them
- get funds from sponsors, select project managers, work out budgets and oversee events
- advise artists and community groups on how to organise projects and help them apply for grants
- distribute arts information to professional artists, organisations and the public
- monitor and evaluate projects.

Arts development officers apply for funding for projects from government, charities or businesses. They advertise for artists to suggest project ideas and help select the winning applicants. Then they follow through projects, working with a community and the artist to deliver the final piece on time and on budget. Some arts development officers work for a particular local government authority or private organisation, but others are freelancers who work with different groups on different projects.

What skills do I need?

You need to be enthusiastic about art and enabling the public to have access to it. Most arts development officers have a degree in arts subjects such as fine art or performing arts, but some have qualifications in event management or community arts. Financial skills, such as knowing how much different artworks cost and where to find funding, and the ability to develop networks of contacts who may be involved in projects, are important to complement practical arts skills.

↑ Murals can brighten city views. This mural was painted as part of a graffiti art project in Bristol, UK.

PROFESSIONAL VIEWPOINT

'The best thing about being an arts development officer is going to an arts event and seeing hundreds of people enjoying it, and knowing that I helped the organisers achieve the funding and gave them advice about employing artists and organising the events.'

Roma Gee, arts development officer, Derbyshire Dales District Council

Curator

A curator's aim is to stop you getting bored when you visit an art exhibition, gallery or museum! A curator decides which paintings, sculptures and other forms of art to put on display. For example, they might choose a retrospective of paintings made through an artist's life or different artworks on a theme. The curator then helps decide how to display the artworks to help people understand or be inspired by them.

↑ A curator has to decide how and where to display each artwork so that the public can see it at its best.

Job description

Curators:

- make decisions about which items to collect and display
- locate suitable works and arrange their loan and transport from other museums, galleries or private collections
- help get funding, for example from businesses, to put on exhibitions or create new galleries
- arrange and display artworks in galleries and other spaces
- maintain catalogues and records of collections
- provide information about artists and their work to help the public interpret and appreciate them
- collaborate with education, fundraising, marketing and conservation departments.

Different types of curator

Curators in contemporary art galleries or other arts venues may only be responsible for temporary exhibitions. They might choose work from applications submitted to the gallery or commission work themselves. Freelance curators organise single exhibitions and events to be shown in larger galleries. Curators employed by the larger galleries manage permanent displays of artworks, build up collections and organise temporary displays using stored or loaned artworks.

PROFESSIONAL VIEWPOINT

'Making sure that people really enjoy our paintings is just as important as the educational aspect. I organise lectures and study days, which are open to everyone. These encourage people to investigate art for themselves.'

Dr Caroline Campbell, Curator of Paintings, The Courtauld Gallery

It's essential to get experience working in art galleries and one of the best ways to do this is by volunteering.

What skills do I need?

Curators need a thorough knowledge of what art the public might want to see now and in the future. Almost all curators hold undergraduate degrees in fine art or art history, and many have postgraduate qualifications in curating. Many will have built up experience in the field by helping to put on exhibitions in small independent galleries before working in large public galleries or museums. Curators should have an understanding of the current market value of artworks as they may need to buy to maintain a collection.

Advertising art director

An advert you glance at for a few seconds on a poster or on TV can make the difference as to whether you buy a product or not. Art directors are responsible for the look of adverts on screen or paper. They work for advertising agencies to help create adverts that promote a client's product, brand or organisation.

↑ As an art director you might see your visual ideas in some unusual places!

In an advertising agency, an art director usually works in a team with a copywriter, who creates the words for an advert. The art director sketches different ideas to match the words. The agency's creative director presents the ideas to clients and once one is chosen, the art director works with artists, photographers and other specialists to express their visual ideas. Advertising art directors are usually hired by creative directors, either in a full-time role or as a freelancer. They can be involved in all of the different advertising platforms, including film, web, posters, magazines and direct mailings.

Art directors:

- work from a brief with a copywriter, generating ideas to present to the client
- work on designs to produce an effective advertising campaign
- commission specialists, such as artists and photographers, to work on projects they have sketched out
- manage projects and work within a budget
- edit the final results for presentation to the client.

→ Art directors work mainly in offices or studios but travel to meet clients and visit television studios or other locations where advertisements are being filmed.

What skills do I need?

Art directors need to come up with lots of visual ideas for adverts and trust their judgement – something wacky or unexpected might be just the look a client wants. There are no set qualifications for becoming an advertising art director, but entrants usually have a degree in art or design. Training is normally in-house, under the supervision of more experienced colleagues. Some agencies require entrants to gain an IPA (Institute of Practitioners in Advertising) foundation certificate, proving their understanding of the advertising industry.

Architect

Any building, from your home to a hospital, begins with a design idea. Architects design new buildings and also make alterations to existing buildings. They draw accurate, detailed plans and models of their designs to help clients check that the designs match their needs. As well as making designs look appealing, architects need to ensure that they are functional, safe and cost no more than a client can afford. Structures also need to be sustainable – for example, by using as little energy as possible.

↑ Architects have to be able to combine imaginative design with technical knowledge.

Job description

Architects:
- discuss the objectives, requirements and budget of a project
- produce detailed workings, drawings and specifications, often using computer-aided design
- consult with other professionals, such as engineers, about the design and safety of structures
- prepare and present reports and design proposals to the client
- specify the type and quality of materials required
- manage projects, co-ordinate the work of contractors and make regular site visits.

What skills do I need?

To become an architect takes at least seven years, so it's a good idea to do some work experience first to make sure it's for you. First, you study for an approved first degree in architecture, known as RIBA Part 1, which takes three or four years. Next, there is a year of supervised practical experience and then two more years studying for a diploma or further degree in architecture, known as RIBA Part 2. You take the final RIBA Part 3 examination after gaining a year's experience in an architect practice.

Different types of architect

Architects may control a project from start to finish, but also work within a team on a small part of a project. Some architects don't just work on buildings. Landscape architects plan and design the layout of open spaces, from parks and gardens to the open spaces in housing estates and cities. Landscape architects also improve the appearance and usability of land affected by mining or motorway construction.

→

Landscape architects must be able to think creatively to transform challenging terrain into beautiful outdoor spaces.

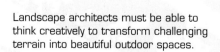

25

Art therapist

Some people have difficulty expressing themselves in words. This might be because they are too young to do so, have lost touch with their feelings or are unable to talk about what is troubling them. Art therapists help people to find ways to express their feelings and work through problems using art, with materials like paint, paper and clay.

Art therapists don't teach clients how to make artwork that looks attractive or artistic. They help clients to experiment with art techniques to express themselves.

Art therapists are sometimes called art psychotherapists. They work with people who suffer from a range of difficulties including mental health problems, behavioural problems or learning disabilities. Art therapists work in a variety of settings, such as psychiatric departments in hospitals, charities, schools or prisons. Art therapists work closely with other professionals including psychologists, nurses, teachers and social workers.

What skills do I need?

Art therapists need to have good communication skills, be non-judgemental and be able to relate to people suffering from physical and mental conditions. They need to be imaginative and flexible in how they maximise benefits to different individuals. Therapists usually have a degree in anything from art to nursing, and then training and qualifications at postgraduate level. Only then are people registered as therapists and allowed to practise on patients. Therapists need to undergo psychotherapy during their training to help them develop the skills and insight to help others.

Job description

Art therapists:
- listen to a client or clients to assess their needs
- plan and carry out a timetable of activities with individuals and groups
- help clients to explore their feelings through art and think about what they produced and why
- write reports for other professionals and case studies
- maintain art therapy space and materials
- work closely with other health professionals and sometimes a client's family or carers.

↑ Art therapists work with a range of people, including refugee children.

Artist

Artists create original pieces of artwork through a variety of media, from charcoal to stained glass. Depending on the medium they specialise in, they may be called a painter, sculptor, printer, collagist or ceramicist. Some, known as performance artists and installation artists, may use a variety of different media to create artworks at particular times or in particular spaces.

➤ Scenic artists paint sets for theatre shows such as plays, ballets and operas.

Job description

Artists:
- generate, research and develop ideas for their projects
- maintain a portfolio and a website of their past work
- write project proposals for galleries, competitions or artist residencies
- apply for funds and grants to support their work
- source materials from suppliers and run a studio
- promote themselves by networking and writing press releases
- liaise with contacts, gallery owners and curators
- negotiate sales or commissions and meet deadlines for their completion.

What skills do I need?

Good technique is important, but success as an artist also means creating pieces that people want. To translate this into sales, you need to make sure your work is seen – for example, by setting up your own website or entering art competitions. Some artists start producing and selling their own work straight after school, without professional qualifications. Most, however, have some formal training such as a foundation or full degree in anything from ceramics to fine art.

Some artists are commissioned by a client to create a piece of art that the client wants, such as portraits of their pets, murals for hospital walls or a sculpture for a shopping centre. Others work independently on their own pieces and earn money selling these through exhibitions in gallery spaces or via websites. Only the most famous make a lucrative career from their art, however, so some artists also take other jobs, like teaching art classes, to supplement their earnings.

↓ Some sculptors specialise in one medium, such as stone, metal, recycled materials or felt.

PROFESSIONAL VIEWPOINT

'You obviously need strong drawing and painting skills. But it's also important to … have a lot of stamina as it is a very physical job. You also need flexibility and creativity as you need to be ready to adapt and change your ways of thinking in order to solve problems, and good time-keeping to meet deadlines.'

Rowan Plinston, scenic artist for the Royal Opera House

Glossary

agent person who manages business and financial matters for an artist, actor, performer or writer

archaeological something related to archaeology, the scientific study of past cultures and the way people lived based on the things they left behind

artefact something made by people, such as pottery, which is of historical interest

brand type of product made by a company under a particular name or a certain, recognisable 'look' of a business or company

brief set of instructions telling someone how to do a piece of work

extra-curricular activities at school or college that are in addition to normal lessons

commission employ someone to make something such as a film or advert

copywriter someone who writes the words for advertisements or publicity material

direct mailing method of advertising in which adverts or letters are mailed to large groups of consumers

edit improve, correct or choose what to leave in and what to cut out of something like a book or a film

engineer person who designs, builds or maintains engines, machines or public works

font word for the type of lettering used in print or on screen

freelance someone who works freelance is self-employed; they are not employed by a particular organisation but instead work for several different ones

genre style or type; crime fiction is a genre of literature

haute couture design and production of high-quality, fashionable clothes by the most well-known fashion designers, often to order for a particular customer

HND Higher National Diploma

layout way in which text and pictures are set out on a page

liaise work with others and keep each other informed, in order to co-ordinate activities and get the outcome all sides want

logo symbol or other small design used by an organisation to identify its products

mass-market something that appeals to the majority of people; for instance, a mass-market film is one that most people would like

media main ways in which people receive information and entertainment, including TV, Internet, radio, newspapers and magazines

perspective the art of drawing objects on a flat surface so as to give the appearance of distance or depth

pitch give a short summary of an idea

portfolio set of pieces of creative work collected by someone to display their skills, especially to a potential employer

retrospective exhibition showing works that represent the development of an artist's career

sponsor person or organisation that provides funds for a project or activity carried out by another

Further information

There are many art jobs out there, as well as the jobs described in this book. To find out about other work you can do in the art world, read other books and check out other relevant websites. Some suggestions are listed on this page. It is also really useful to talk to careers advisers at school or college, and attend careers and college or university fairs, to find out about the options out there. The earlier you check out your options and discover what will help you get those jobs, the sooner you will be able to start doing the extra-curricular things, like volunteering at a local art gallery, that will help you.

Books

Art (Jobs if you like...), Charlotte Guillain, Raintree, 2013

Choosing Your A Levels: and other academic options, Cerys Evans, Trotman, 2012

What Do Authors and Illustrators Do? (Two Books in One), Eileen Christelow, Houghton Mifflin Harcourt, 2013

Being a Fashion Stylist (On the Radar: Awesome Jobs), Isabel Thomas, Lerner Publications, 2012

Working in Creative & Performing Arts, Babcock Lifeskills, 2011

Wildlife Photographer (The Coolest Jobs on the Planet), Gerrit Vyn, Gareth Stevens Publishing, 2009

Websites

www.theartcareerproject.com/art-as-a-career
This site has a list of careers in art with information about each of them, from graphic designers and graffiti artists to medical illustrators and muralists.

www.creative-choices.co.uk
On this site, you can choose an arts discipline from the 'Choose a creative sector' pull-down menu to find career information and advice from working artists

www.prospects.ac.uk/types_of_jobs_creative_arts_and_design.htm
This website is a useful guide to your job options. It is aimed at art and design students and it gives a clear idea of what routes to take for many art and design careers. There is also a list of resources and contacts on this site.

www.creativeskillset.org/careers
This website has information about a variety of industries and career paths that might interest you, under headings such as Advertising, Photo Imaging and Publishing.

Index

advertising 5, 14, 17, 22, 23

advertising art directors 22–23

agents 6, 7

architects 24–25

art conservators 8–9

art development officers 18–19

art foundation 7, 10, 15, 23, 29

art galleries 9, 13, 21, 31

art history 9, 12, 13, 21

art teachers 12–13

art therapists 26–27

artists 4, 5, 9, 12, 18, 19, 20, 22, 23, 28–29

artwork 5, 8, 9, 18, 19, 20, 21, 28

budgets 6, 17, 18

buildings 24, 25

ceramicists 28

ceramics 9, 12, 29

clothing 10

computer graphics 6

costume design 5, 11

curators 20-21

deadlines 6, 16, 17, 28

degree 5, 7, 9, 10, 13, 15, 17, 19, 21, 23, 25, 27, 29

drawing 6, 10, 12

exhibitions 4, 5, 17, 18, 20, 21, 29

experience 9, 15, 17, 21, 25

fashion 7, 10, 11

fashion designers 10–11

fine art 7, 9, 19, 21, 29

freelance 7

galleries 5, 9, 12, 13, 20, 21, 28, 29

graphic designers 16–17

haute couture 11

HND 7, 10, 15, 17

illustration 6, 7, 17

illustrators 6–7

installation artists 28

landscape architects 25

murals 18, 19, 29

museums 5, 9, 20, 21

painters 28

painting 4, 6, 9, 12, 13, 20, 21, 29

performance artists 28

photographers 14–15

photography 14, 15, 17, 22, 23

photojournalism 14, 15

picture books 6, 7

printers 17, 28

psychotherapists 26

sculptors 28

sculpture 12, 18, 20, 29

textiles 9, 10

visual art 7, 9, 17

websites 14, 17, 29, 31